IMAGES OF ENGLAND

GLOUCESTERSHIRE
PUBS AND BREWERIES

Geoff Sandles

Cheers,   Tim Edgell.

IMAGES OF ENGLAND

GLOUCESTERSHIRE
PUBS AND BREWERIES

TIM EDGELL AND GEOFF SANDLES

TEMPUS

For Sarah, Hope and Isabella, Mum and Dad.

For Kathy and Sophie (thanks for letting me use my computer!).

Frontispiece: 'Blessings of your heart, you brew good ale', *Two Gentlemen of Verona*, Act III, Scene I. William Shakespeare and the authors of this book have one thing in common: they never drank Stroud Brewery Cotswold Beers! William Shakespeare would have been nearly 400 years old when the brewery was thriving and, unfortunately, Geoff and Tim were born too late.

First published 2005

Tempus Publishing Limited
The Mill, Brimscombe Port,
Stroud, Gloucestershire, GL5 2QG
www.tempus-publishing.com

© Tim Edgell and Geoff Sandles, 2005

The right of Tim Edgell and Geoff Sandles to be identified
as the Authors of this work has been asserted in accordance
with the Copyrights, Designs and Patents Act 1988.

British Library Cataloguing in Publication Data.
A catalogue record for this book is available from the British Library.

ISBN 0 7524 3524 8

Typesetting and origination by Tempus Publishing Limited.
Printed in Great Britain.

Contents

Introduction

In 1885 a gentleman by the name of Alfred Barnard wrote a book called *The Noted Breweries of Great Britain*. Alfred travelled England, Scotland and Wales in search of breweries both in towns and in the countryside. He obviously loved his beer and his lengthy descriptions of the breweries seem to have been inspired by the consumption of several pints of the finest ale. On his visit to the Nailsworth Brewery he wrote:

> We found the bitter ale simply delicious, full of life, well flavoured with hops, and for brightness and condition quite up to the standard of the London and Burton ales. Stout has always been a speciality of this brewery, its fame having long since reached almost every village and town of Gloucestershire. We sampled the extra stout, which we found to be a rich drink, full of body, and of highly nutritious qualities. Of the bottled pale ale and porters we can also speak in unqualified terms of praise.

In fact, in 1885, Alfred Barnard could have gone to any market town in Gloucestershire where he would have found at least one small family-owned brewery to wax lyrical about. Some pubs were making home-brewed ales for consumption on the premises, other breweries were supplying beer for the family or take-home trade and the commercial breweries were actively buying pubs to ensure that they had guaranteed outlets for their beers.

As time went by, some of the more successful family brewers sought to expand by becoming public companies. In 1888 Gardners Original Brewery in Cheltenham, for example, released 12,000 Ordinary Shares at £5 each to raise £217,310 for the purchase of the brewery and its 123 public houses and hotels. Cheltenham Original Brewery was fitted with the most up-to-date brewing equipment and because the brewery used the finest available ingredients, and was meticulously cleaned after each brew, the resultant beers were superb and widely sought after. In contrast, some of the common and small family breweries found it difficult to brew consistently good beer. Burdened with inconsistent quality, increased taxes on beer and the declaration of war against Germany in 1914 it is hardly surprising that so many country breweries were taken over. Alfred Barnard's beloved Nailsworth Brewery was amalgamated with the Cheltenham Brewery in 1908. Further acquisitions included Green's Brewery at Stow-on-the-Wold and Tayler's Cotswold Brewery in Northleach.

The Stroud Brewery Co. also realised that by purchasing the struggling breweries they could acquire their pubs cheaply and thus increase the guaranteed outlets for their own beers. Very few of these acquisitions were hostile takeovers.

In 1945 the Cheltenham Brewery acquired the Hereford & Tredegar Brewery Ltd and as a result changed its name to the Cheltenham & Hereford Brewery Ltd. Meanwhile, the Stroud Brewery had developed into one of the most important regional breweries in the west of England. In 1958 the two breweries merged to form West Country Breweries.

1,275 pubs were tied to West Country Breweries extending into ten counties, stretching from Radnorshire to Wiltshire and Monmouthshire to Worcestershire. West Country Breweries adopted the castle trademark of the Cheltenham Brewery and attractive ceramic plaques were inlaid into the walls of their pubs proclaiming that their ales were the 'Best in the West'.

By the late 1950s the taste in beer was slowly changing from traditional cask beer to bottled and container beer. Stroud Brewery had invested considerable amounts of money into their bottling plant and bottled beer accounted for 40 per cent of total production. Double Gloster keg beer was also introduced at this time and proved surprisingly popular.

In 1963 Whitbread & Co. took over West Country Breweries. To begin with, the new ownership brought little change but gradually West Country signs were replaced with Whitbread ones and by 1967 brewing at the Stroud Brewery had ceased. The new corporate Whitbread brands of the early 1970s were heavily advertised on the television. Tankard and Trophy keg beer replaced Double Gloster and the traditional draught beers of the Stroud and Cheltenham breweries were phased out. Only West Country Pale Ale remained. Pale Ale (PA) had an original gravity (OG) of 1030 which made it one of the weakest commercial beers in the country.

West Country Breweries merged with Flowers in 1968 to become Whitbread Flowers. The real Flowers Stratford-upon-Avon brewery was closed down. Cheltenham became the ersatz Flowers Brewery in 1991. The last brew of West Country PA took place in 1997. In the final year of operation the Cheltenham brewery was producing beers like Flowers Original and Flowers IPA along with a few special beers that were very highly regarded by beer drinkers.

The Campaign for Real Ale (CAMRA) was formed in the early 1970s when a few like-minded beer drinkers realised that large companies like Whitbread were heavily advertising their keg beers while trying to phase out their naturally conditioned cask ales. CAMRA coined the phrase 'real ale' to describe the old-fashioned traditional beer that was not subjected to the pasteurisation, filtration and excessive chilling which typified keg beers.

Despite Whitbread's best efforts, quality breweries continue to thrive in Gloucestershire. Tucked away in a secluded picturesque Cotswold valley near Stow-on-the-Wold is the privately owned Donnington Brewery. This superb brewery was established in 1865 and is still producing beer for its small estate of fifteen pubs to this day. Donnington is the archetypal traditional brewery and its beers have long been sought after by real-ale enthusiasts. Alfred Barnard would feel very much at home drinking Donnington Ales.

In fact, if Alfred were alive today no doubt he would be seeking out beers brewed in Gloucestershire from the new generation of breweries. Freeminer, Goffs, Home County, Stanway, Uley, Whittingtons and Wickwar Breweries all produce truly superb traditional beer which Mr Barnard would only be too happy to endorse.

When the Whitbread Flowers brewery finally closed in 1997 it was thought that brewing had come to an end in Cheltenham. However, plans are now well in advance to open a micro-brewery in the town.

Gloucestershire breweries are alive and well. Let's drink to that.

About the Authors

Tim Edgell and Geoff Sandles share a passion for beer. They are both members of CAMRA and the Brewery History Society. Geoff is currently the editor of the CAMRA newsletter *The Tippler* which can be regularly seen in real-ale pubs in the county of Gloucestershire. Geoff has done extensive research into the history of pubs in Gloucestershire and has put the information onto his website *www.gloucestershirepubs.co.uk*. Tim actively collects brewery memorabilia from Gloucestershire breweries, especially in the Stroud area. He can be contacted on 01453 835405, email: *stroudbrewerytim@btinternet.com*.

Acknowledgements

Special thanks go to Annie Blick (Peckhams Photographers, Stroud), John Saunders (Past & Present Books, Coleford) and Howard Beard for their continuous supply of images and help over a long period. Also thanks to English Heritage.NMR.

Many thanks to the following:

Chris and Geraldine Ames, Derek Arthurs, John Astridge, Andrew and Lucy Atkins, Mark Bailey, Peter Ballantyne, Jim Barge, Janet Bartlett, Chris Beaumont, Jerry Biggs, Vernon Bland, Sarah Bull, Don Burgess, Roy and Betty Close, Vic Cole, Alice Cook, Cotswold District Council, Crown Copyright.NMR, Mick Croxford, Tim Curr, Diana Dalton, Rob and Leslie Davis, *Dursley Gazette*, Mr P. Gadsden, Keith Gardiner, Hayden and Susan Gardiner, Mike Gatenby, Freda Gittos, *Gloucestershire Echo*, Jack Godsell, Mike Goodenough (Inprint Books), Edward Godsell, Peter Grace, Howard Griffiths, David Hanks, Steve Harker, Eric Harper, Peter Harris, Mike and Margaret Hawkes, Andrew Helme, Stuart and Joyce Hodge, Adrian Holloway, Martin and Brian Hunt, Mary Isaac, Joy Jellings, Malcolm Jones, Ken Kerley, Dave Lewis, Alf Lovell, Anne Makemson, Andy Mears, Louisa Merlock, Wilf Merrett, Mike Mills, Minchinhampton Archives, Sid Mosdell, David Morris, Chris Mortimer (at Malthouse Antiques), Walter Monk, Brian Moss, Russell Murfitt, Nailsworth Archives, Roger Neale, Keith Osborne, Graham and Sheila Owen, Neil Parkhouse Collection (at Lightmoor Books), Amber Patrick, Robert Pearce, Robin and Julian Pearce, Ray Penny, Tim Petchey, Patrick Phair, Humphrey Phelps, Steve Pritchard, Penny Proudfoot, Ruth Pyecroft, Mick Rafferty, Nick Redman, Chris Rose, Mr H. Sambell (Butts Photography), Colin Savage, David Springate, Neil Stevenson (National Monument Record, Swindon), Mark Steeds, Joe Stevens, Stow Library and The Civic Society, David Tandy, Dave Tate, Coralie Taylor, Alec Thomas, John Thornell, Rich Tucker, Les Tuffley, Di Wall, Mike Ward, Phil Warn, Michael Wilkes, Kevan Witt, Reg Woolford, Wotton Under Edge Archives, Chas Wright.

Bibliography

200 years of brewing in the West Country, West Country Brewery Holdings Ltd
A Century of British Brewers 1890-1990, Norman Barber (Brewery History Society)
The English Pub – A history, Peter Haydon (Robert Hale Ltd)
You Brew Good Ale – A history of small-scale brewing, Ian P. Peaty (Sutton Publishing)
The Tippler – CAMRA Gloucestershire newsletter
What's Brewing – CAMRA national newsletter

Useful Websites

www.camra.org.uk
www.freeminer.com
www.goffs.biz
www.gloucestershirepubs.co.uk
www.stanwaybrewery.co.uk
www.stroudvalleybreweries.co.uk
www.uleybrewery.com
www.whittingtonsbrewery.co.uk
www.wickwarbrewing.co.uk

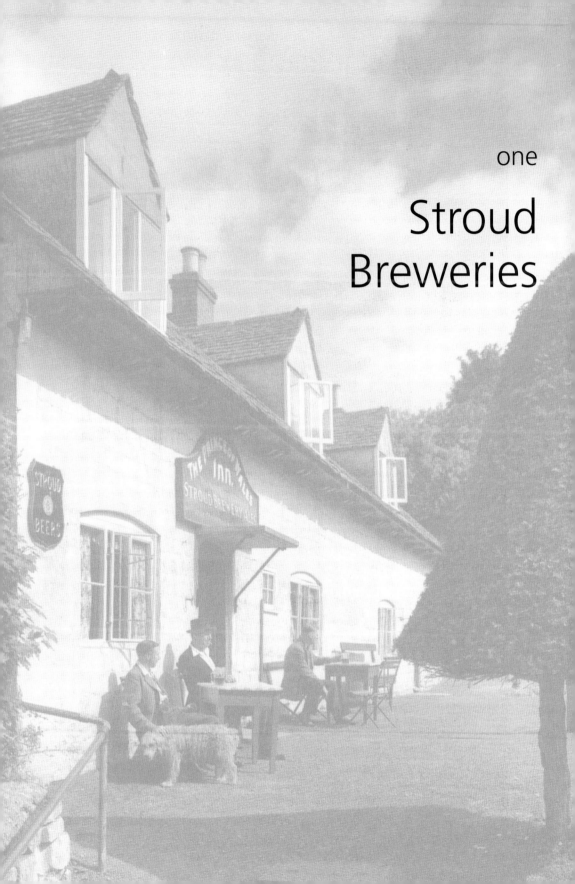

one

Stroud
Breweries

Left: Joseph Watts, the sole proprietor of the Stroud Brewery from 1819, was a prominent and influential character and a devout Christian. When returning from Sunday church one day a beggar walked up to Mr Watts demanding money. Upon receiving the princely sum of sixpence the beggar thanked Mr Watts and assured him that his money would be well spent on two or three pints of his finest Stroud Ales.

Below: Teddy Wilkins, an employee, composed a poem consisting of 84 stanzas devoted entirely to the Stroud Brewery. It was hardly a literary masterpiece: *When going, one day, to my employ, I met a wagon load full of joy/It made me thirsty to see it – for why? – it came from Watt's Brewery.* Teddy died in 1825 from the effects of hard drinking. Not really a good advert for the company.

The Stroud Brewery chimney, built in 1901, was a prominent landmark in the town. A new recruit to the brewery in 1905 was young lad called William Stafford. Bill was bet by one of his fellow workers that he would not climb to the top. The opportunity came one day when steeplejacks maintaining the chimney went for an early dinner. Bill climbed to the top and won his bet.

Stroud Brewery had two malthouses in the town. The malthouse in the photograph was across the road from the brewery just below the Bell Hotel. Part of the brickwork remains to this day. The main A46 through Stroud was realigned in 1966 to its present route through Merrywalks. The other malthouse was on the opposite side of the railway viaduct and is currently a nightclub and an indoor bowls centre.

The Stroud Brewery offices were decorated for the Coronation of King George V on 22 June 1911. Electric lighting was a relatively new invention.

The Stroud Brewery office buildings were splendidly decorated for the 1953 Coronation. The design was by Michael Wearran and John Cook and their work resulted in an illuminated display that featured marching soldiers and a golden stagecoach with revolving wheels. Stroud Brewery also brewed a Strong Coronation Ale for the occasion which was on sale in public bars at 1s 9d per half-pint bottle.

Barley needs to be converted into malt before it is suitable for brewing. Briefly, it is steeped in water, allowed to germinate and then carefully dried so that the natural sugars can be used in the brewing process. The process requires a high degree of skill as the resultant beer is entirely dependent on the quality of the malted barley.

Crushed malt is added to the mash tun where it is mixed with hot liquor (brewers never call it water!). The resultant mixture, resembling a thick porridge, is allowed to stand for about two hours. The mash is constantly sprayed or sparged with hot liquor to maximise the amount of natural sugars extracted from the malt into the liquid wort. Temperature control is crucial throughout.

Left: The sweet liquid or wort is then run off into a copper. The spent grains in the mash tun are disposed of and used for cattle feed. In the copper the wort is vigorously boiled with a selection of hops. The character and bitterness of the beer is dependent on the type and amount of hops used. Boiling kills off the bacteria in the wort and the hops act as a preservative.

After rapid cooling fresh yeast is added. Yeast is made up of millions of individual microscopic organisms which display frantic biochemical activity when they come into contact with the sugar-rich wort. Fermentation is a critical part of the brewing process and it is essential that all the fermentation vessels and pipes are kept scrupulously clean to prevent yeast infection which could lead to obnoxious flavours in the finished beer.

To ensure that the beer was clear from excess sediment when it entered the casks Stroud Brewery kept the fermenting beer in conditioning tanks for a time. Here finings were added to drag the yeast particles to the bottom of the tank. Finings, incidentally, are a natural additive made from the swim bladders of sturgeon fish.

By the late 1940s Stroud Brewery had invested considerable capital into their automated bottling plant. Ironically the quality of beer was probably better when the beers were bottled manually, as seen above. In the 1920s the original gravity of the beer was higher and because it was not subjected to pasteurisation the bottled beer was more traditional in character.

The automated bottling hall at Salmon Springs must have been a very noisy place to work with the constant chinking and rattling of bottles as they passed by on rollers and conveyors to be washed, filled, labelled, crown corked and put into crates automatically.

Above: The bottles were subject to the process of pasteurisation which sterilised the beer and changed its flavour significantly. All traces of yeast were killed off in the process and the resultant beer was clear, sparkling and every last drop could be poured from the glass. Beer aficionados maintain that a better-tasting beer is obtained by leaving some yeast in the bottle but the Stroud Brewery Co. clearly thought otherwise!

Right: In June 1947 a new beer bottle was introduced with the Stroud Brewery Co. logo fired onto the glass. Although considerably more expensive than the standard bottle it was thought that economies could be achieved by the elimination of paper labels. Different coloured crown corks were used for All Bright (gold), Home Brewed (blue), Stout (brown), Guinness (green), Worthington (grey) and Bass (red).

Clogs were traditionally worn in the bottling hall to avoid cuts from smashed bottles but steel-capped boots had replaced clogs by the late 1950s. The workers at the Stroud Brewery bottling plant at Salmon Springs were given an allowance of two pint bottles of beer every day.

The Stroud Brewery Co. was not just passionate about beer. They also had a Wines & Spirits Department and took pride in selecting the very best vintages. In 1948 Jack Hillier of the department was sent to London for three months to learn about high-class wines. The Wines & Spirits Department also had a foreman who was given the nickname of 'Fatty' Bennett, on account of his weight.

Stroud Brewery had their own cooper's shop, where new casks were made and old ones repaired. A cooper had to serve an apprenticeship from five to seven years and he was then initiated into the brewery by a ceremony known as 'trussing.' He was put into an empty barrel and loose shavings and beer were poured over him, all while the barrel was being pushed and noisily banged by his fellow workers.

Guinness Extra Stout, which was brewed at the Dublin Brewery, was sent in barrels to many breweries in England for bottling, including this one. Stroud Brewery also bottled Worthington and Bass beers.

The Stroud Brewery bought two Halford lorries in 1911. They were considerably speedier than the horse-drawn drays that they replaced but with solid tyres, an open cab, and only acetylene lamps for illumination they were hardly luxury modes of transport. The drivers, Mr J. Ellicott, Mr A. Marsh and Mr G.M. Taylor, were protected from adverse weather conditions by simple canvas sheeting. The Halfords were requisitioned by the War Office in 1914.

From 1925 Stroud Brewery purchased a number of Thornycroft petrol lorries which gave many years of reliable service. In October 1928 an unfortunate incident occurred when the head brewer of the Stroud Brewery, Mr J.D. Wilson, died in a motoring accident in London Road, Stroud. Ironically, a motor lorry belonging to the Stroud Brewery Co. was responsible for the tragedy having 'skidded and passed over him'.

By 1947 the Stroud Brewery had a fleet of twenty-two vehicles and, with their distinctive colours of red and blue, they were a familiar sight over a wide area. A seventeen-year-old Thornycroft, No. 24, had run up over 300,000 miles by this time and it was still giving reliable service. Its driver was Gilbert Bingham who had been given a long-service award by the company.

This peculiar-looking Scammell mechanical horse, driven by Joe Ruck, must have travelled thousands of miles while never actually being further than three-quarters of a mile away from the Stroud Brewery. The glass-lined tanks were used to transport All Bright Pale Ale direct from the conditioning tanks at the brewery to the automated bottling plant at Salmon Springs.

Left: The brick-built Ludlow Green Inn near Ruscombe, one-and-a-half miles to the north-west of Stroud, was tied to the nearby Godsell's Brewery until 1928 when it became a Stroud Brewery pub. The locals at the pub won the Cribbage knock-out cup for the 1952 season. George Reynolds was the landlord. The Ludlow Green Inn had closed by 1971.

Fred Willis wrote a poem about the Yew Tree Inn at Walls Quarry near Brimscombe in 1927. The last verse went:

A genial host and hostess keep the friendly spirit going
No matter how the world may wag, or what is paid or owing
How sweet it is to find a spot where perfect peace is dwelling
I'll never forget the Yew Tree, or George and Laura Snelling!

The Victoria Inn was located on the banks of the Stroudwater Canal above the lock at Dudbridge. James Clarke was landlord in early Edwardian times and his daughter, Annie, had taken over the licence by 1939. Annie was born in the house in 1893.

The Stroud Brewery Co. took a great deal of pride in their pubs. Each year they had a gardens competition. In 1947 the top prize of £30 was awarded to the Pilot Inn at Hardwicke. Despite his wonderful topiary skills, the landlord of the Prince of Wales in Slad Road, Stroud failed to win a prize.

"BY YOUR LEAVE, PLEASE!"

Above: Passengers waiting for their train at Stroud GWR station were either delighted or disgusted by the aroma of malted barley and boiling hops emanating from the Stroud Brewery. Space was at a premium at the cramped brewery site. One of the arches of the railway viaduct was used as the cask-washing stores.

Left: As early as 1926 Stroud Brewery was chilling and carbonating their bottled beers. All Bright bottled beer was, according to the brewery, 'brilliant in colour, properly aerated, and could be drunk to the last drop'. Beer drinkers tended to opt for the new bottled beer in preference to naturally conditioned.

A late 1950s promotional display of Stroud Brewery bottled beers complete with a guide to the Cotswolds and a packet of 'Players Please' cigarettes! It seems incredible in these enlightened times that cigarettes were used in advertising. Also note the peeling wallpaper used as a backdrop.

The self-proclaimed 'formidable' Maltsters Skittle Team taken in the late 1950s. Back row, from left to right: Eddie Smith, Lionel Rook, Stan Mills (foreman at Salmon Springs Brewery), Harry Vick, Jim 'Taffy' Cullen. Front row: Dick Brown (foreman at Stroud Brewery Malthouse), George Cook, Don Smith, Jim Long.

Almost every pub used to have one – a darts team. The Box Inn was a wonderful village local and this was their ace team from the 1940s. From left to right, standing: Billy Williams, Billy Humphries, Bill Lusty, Ted Grey, Ray Merretts, Percy Ind (with beer in hand), Albert Ind, Jim Spry, Sam Rodway, Anthony Vanston, Charles Churchley. Crouching in front: Peter Mills, Tom Llewellyn, Wally Poole, Owen Baker.

In 1880 the average original gravity of beer was 1057. In 1939 it had fallen to 1041. By 1943 the average beer strength was 1034.3 OG. The Stroud Brewery may have claimed to 'meet the needs of the age' on their 1939 Stroud carnival float but beer drinkers certainly got a better deal in 1880.

The motor lorry allowed breweries to acquire pubs a considerable distance from the brewery. The pubs of the Stroud Brewery eventually extended into a large proportion of Gloucestershire and Wiltshire, with outposts in Oxfordshire, Herefordshire and Monmouthshire. The Starting Gate was a Hereford pub.

The Gardener's Rest at Cashes Green was opened on 15 August 1956. It was one of the last new public houses to be commissioned by the Stroud Brewery and was designed by architects H.R. Robinson. In the early 1960s the Gardener's Rest won the prestigious Stroud Darts League knockout competition, held in the Stroud Subscription Rooms.

Left: Nearly all the pubs in the 1950s and '60s had a separate bar and lounge. In the 1970s and '80s interior walls were knocked down so that brewers could increase the trading area of the pub. Multi-roomed pubs are now rare. The Gardener's Rest is one of the few pubs to retain its bar and lounge. New legislation restricting smoking in public spaces could possibly bring back separate smoking rooms.

two

Cheltenham Breweries

Left: Mr John Gardner started brewing in Cheltenham High Street in 1760. Upon his death the brewery was bequeathed to his son-in-law James Agg. James changed his name to Agg-Gardner to perpetuate the name and his son, James Tynte Agg-Gardner, became sole proprietor of Gardner's Original Brewery from 1858-88. After registration as a Limited Liability Company in 1888 R.T. Agg-Gardner (pictured) became the chairman. He was also Cheltenham's MP.

Below: In 1850 the Fleece Hotel was a high-class commercial and coaching inn run by a Mr Yearsley. Like his predecessor, Thomas Hurlston, Mr Yearsley was a wine merchant 'who possesses a stock of the choicest vintages, the excellence of which has occasioned a well-earned celebrity to attach to this hotel'. The Gardner's beer was good too!

It is interesting to note the size of the wooden fermenting vessels in the Cheltenham Brewery. These were possibly used for storing porter which needed a time to mature. The London brewers had installed massive vessels. In October 1814 a 22ft high vat containing 3,555 barrels of porter burst. Eight people died and several houses were demolished in the flood.

Right: A devastating fire took place at the brewery in 1897 when all the main buildings were destroyed. Only the cellars remained. When the brewery was rebuilt the large fermenting vessels were replaced with smaller ones. The fashion for pale and amber ales, similar to those brewed at Burton upon Trent, meant that different styles of beer could be brewed at the brewery. Variety had replaced volume.

After the fire the Cheltenham Original Brewery was rebuilt under the supervision of its chairman, Sir James Agg-Gardner MP, and it reopened in 1898. The new brewery was recognised as being as 'one of the most excellently equipped in England, and moreover it was built with the wise foresight of allowing considerable expansion without great expense'.

Left: After the reconstruction each department in the brewery was equipped with the most up-to-date plant known in the brewing industry. A special suction plant was installed which sucked the malt from the malthouse to the brewery, a distance of some 300 yards, and the company went to great lengths to ensure absolute cleanliness throughout the brewing process.

These horse-drawn carriages are decked out for the Coronation of Edward VII on 9 August 1902. The maltings of the Cheltenham Original Brewery were only four years old when the photograph was taken. The façade of the old maltings will be a dominant feature of the new 'Brewery' retail development.

The sign above the pub, in this pictorial advertisement, suggests that the name was the Three Horseshoes. Cheltenham Original Brewery did have a pub called the Three Horseshoes but it was just outside the brewery gates in Henrietta Street – hardly hunting country!

The horse-drawn brewery drays were an efficient method of transport, as long as the pubs they delivered beer to were located near the brewery. As pubs were acquired further away from Cheltenham a fleet of motor lorries were used for deliveries and the horse-drawn vehicles were eventually withdrawn.

Sentinel steam lorries were used by the Cheltenham Original Brewery for only a short period of time as the advent of the petrol lorry effectively killed the use of steam. However, the early petrol brewery drays were notoriously temperamental and journeys up the Cotswold escarpment were often interrupted with boiling radiators before the summit was even reached. The Cheltenham Brewery also boasted the first vehicle with pneumatic tyres in Gloucestershire.

In 1856 the wonderfully named D.J. Crump is listed as a brewer at the Wheatsheaf in Old Bath Road, Leckhampton. Cheltenham Original Brewery had acquired the pub by 1891 and it was later completely rebuilt by the company. Judging by the large wooden hogshead barrels on the dray lorry the Wheatsheaf was a beer-drinker's pub – a hogshead contained 54 gallons.

The three-wheeled tractor unit was developed by railway companies in the late 1920s to utilise existing horse trailers. These peculiar-looking articulated mechanical horses were ideally suited for use in town delivery traffic. With a 16ft trailer they could turn a full circle in just 19ft.

The attractive and colourful Best in the West ceramic plaques featuring the castle trademark of the Cheltenham Brewery first started being inlaid into pub walls in the 1930s. The early Cheltenham Ales plaques were replaced with a slightly modified design in 1947 with the words: Cheltenham & Hereford Ales. These, in turn, were replaced with the familiar West Country Ales plaques of which many survive to this day.

Changing the names of public houses is sometimes a contentious issue, especially when a traditional pub name is altered for no apparent reason. There were no complaints when Whitbread changed the name of several pubs called the New Inn in Gloucestershire in the early 1970s. The New Inn at Gretton became the Bugatti – named after the nearby Prescott Hill Climb and its association with the Bugatti motor car.

West Country Breweries were a large regional brewery in the early 1960s and spent a lot of money advertising their beers. They also sponsored events such as the Bugatti Owners Club international rally. The slogan 'Enjoy your West Country Beers' could be seen on beer mats, trays and other point of sale material.

Cricket was a popular recreational sport for brewery staff, particularly those employed at the Stroud Brewery. The chairman of the company in 1946, Lt-Col. Kenneth Godsell, often captained the brewery cricket team and they played in front of his Stratford House residence. Colonel Godsell specialised as a bowler and his best figures were 6 for 5 in 1930. Walter Lionel Powell, head brewer, achieved a hat trick in 1939.

Left: In a cleverly worded message, Col. W.H. Whitbread, in a book to celebrate the joint bicentenary of the Cheltenham and Hereford Breweries, wrote: 'Two hundred years after their separate foundation the breweries find it advisable to compete no longer, but to combine and exchange their goods and experience and re-equip their breweries and houses to meet modern conditions together'.

Above: West Country Breweries had a hugely talented inn-sign painting department, one of the best in the land. Seated in the foreground is Mike Hawkes, in whose handsome image is the Pilot on the sign. In front of the Royal George sign are Bob Simmonds (seated) and John 'Rembrandt' Cook.

Right: The Gamecock Inn was a Regency building on the corner of Monson Avenue and St Margarets Road. It was demolished to make way for the West Country Breweries office block in the early 1960s. The replacement Gamecock was on the ground floor. It served as the brewery tap but had no traditional beer. Discerning drinkers preferred the nearby Stonehouse Inn. The Gamecock was renamed the Brewery Tap in the 1980s.

Above: Sometime in 1966, architectural drawings were submitted to Cheltenham Borough Council. A great swathe of the northern side was razed to the ground including the Fleece Hotel, Brewery Offices and the Grammar School. It was replaced by a concrete shopping precinct.

Left: In the late 1950s and early '60s draught beers produced at the West Country Brewery included Cheltenham Mild Ale, Cheltenham Bitter and Cheltenham Pale Ale. In the 1970s most of the beer production was Trophy Bitter, a keg beer. Whitbread PA was the only West Country beer left. The situation improved in the early 1990s when the Cheltenham Brewery brewed some excellent specialist one-off brews.

Above: In March 1980 the Whitbread
Cheltenham Brewery introduced a
new cask beer called Flowers Bitter. A
Whitbread spokesman told the Campaign
for Real Ale: 'We feel there is a market
for a cask beer, particularly one with the
Flowers name'. He forgot to mention that
Whitbread had already closed down the
real Flowers Brewery in Stratford upon
Avon in 1968.

Right: At the beginning of 1998 it seemed
probable that the Whitbread South West
HQ in Monson Avenue had a secure
future. Reorganisation within the company
had closed two regional headquarters
and Monson Avenue had been selected
to have a responsibility for a larger area.
Regrettably, in August 2000 Whitbread
closed the HQ. It was demolished four
years later.

Above: In the last years of operation at the Cheltenham Brewery, Whitbread employed a team of seventy staff. Martin McDonnell is seen here supervising the mash. The mash tun could handle 14 tons of malt in each brew and was often used twice a day. Around 2,000 casks a day could be brewed at Cheltenham which is equivalent to some 400,000 pints. (Courtesy of the *Gloucestershire Echo*)

Left: The coppers at the Cheltenham Brewery were used for boiling the liquid wort with hops. Water, or liquor, is the main ingredient of beer. The Cheltenham Brewery used between 97 million and 100 million gallons of water a year. The brewing liquor must be pure and free from contamination. All the water used for brewing came from the Northfield Spring, which feeds the Hewletts reservoir.

Right: Until recently excise duty was paid on the specific gravity of the wort before fermentation. The higher the gravity the higher the tax paid. Pete Watts checks the potential strength of a brew of Flowers Original Bitter using a hydrometer, a graduated float used for measuring the amount of sugar in a solution. The original gravity was expressed as, say, 1040 OG. (Courtesy of the *Gloucestershire Echo*)

Below: In 1997 Mike Ward was the quality control technician at the Flowers Brewery in Cheltenham. Mike told the *Gloucestershire Echo*: 'a lot of people probably think it's the best job in the world but tasting is only a small part of what we do – and you have to spit the beer out'. The rumours that the department suffered from a constant shortage of buckets are probably not true. (Courtesy of the *Gloucestershire Echo*)

Above: A new processing plant was installed at the Cheltenham Flowers Brewery in 1989. Mayor Eric Phillips pushes the button watched by brewery manager David Hudson and retired brewery worker Alfie Taylor. The beer used as a toast was probably Flowers Original Bitter. (Courtesy of the *Gloucestershire Echo*)

Left: The brewery yard at Cheltenham was once a scene of frenetic activity with dozens of dray lorries being loaded with barrels of beer for distribution to pubs. When Whitbread Flowers opened a new transport depot in Barnwood in 1980 beer was taken in bulk from the brewery and distributed from there. Keith Lamb is seen stacking empty casks at the Cheltenham Brewery in 1997. (Courtesy of the *Gloucestershire Echo*)

When West Country Breweries opened a new pub in the Hesters Way estate in Cheltenham in the late 1950s it was given the name the Tankard and Castle, a reference to the trademarks of the Stroud and Cheltenham Breweries. In the 1980s, in an attempt to revitalise the troublesome pub, it was renamed the Goat and Bicycle and then to Winners No. 1. The pub has now been demolished.

Interior of the Tankard and Castle. In their bicentenary book the managing directors of West Country Breweries wrote: 'Standing on the threshold of our third century we look back with pride on 200 changing years and forward with confidence to a future of challenging times. In this revolution it is inevitable that some of the smaller houses will disappear and be replaced by modern premises better equipped to cater for forthcoming generations'.

For years the Cheltenham Brewery was synonymous with just one beer: West Country Pale Ale, 1030 OG. CAMRA described the beer as 'a thin bitter' in their 1976 *Good Beer Guide*. The demand for Pale Ale declined as the public opted for stronger beers and the last brew was made in February 1997. Pete Thick enjoys his last pint of Pale Ale at the Somerset Arms in Cheltenham. (Courtesy of the *Gloucestershire Echo*)

Opposite below: In August 1998 the Gloucestershire branch of CAMRA collected about 6,000 signatures in a petition opposing plans to close the Flowers Brewery in Cheltenham. Chairman Tony Aburrow (left) is pictured with Helen and Colin Bolton and Trevor Carter. Campaigning had also taken place at the CAMRA Cotswold Beer Festival in July where Cheltenham-brewed Flowers IPA and Original were on offer for the last time. (Courtesy of the *Gloucestershire Echo*)

Right: In January 1998 a report in *The Guardian* claimed that Whitbread were considering closing the Flowers Brewery in Cheltenham. At the time a spokeswoman for Whitbread declined to say that the rumours were true. She said: 'That's market rumour and speculation and we won't comment. Time and time again it's come up and we never comment on it'. (Courtesy of the *Gloucestershire Echo*)

The last brew at the Cheltenham Brewery took place on 19 August 1998. Ironically this was exactly 100 years after the brewery had reopened after the disastrous fire in 1897. Needless to say there were no centenary celebrations. The brewery was demolished in 2004 but the old tower brew house will be retained in the new development. (Courtesy of the *Gloucestershire Echo*)

Above: The Albion Brewery was located in Gloucester Road near the junction with the High Street. The Gas Works were opposite. In this early lithograph Richard Masters and Christie & Co. were offering 'Porter, Ale and Table Beer'. The business was later acquired by Harris & Leighton. The buildings were demolished in around 1873 and the site was developed as the Cattle Market. Apparently the locals could not differentiate between the unique smell of malted barley and gas and the replacement aroma of cow manure and gas!

RIGHTON & CO.,

Anchor Brewery,

WARWICK PLACE, CHELTENHAM.

ALE AND PORTER BREWERS,

SPECIALLY BREWED FROM THE TOWN WATER.

WINE AND SPIRIT MERCHANTS

AND

MINERAL WATER MANUFACTURERS.

FAMILIES SUPPLIED WITH CASKS OF ALL SIZES.

Opposite below: In 1850 the Anchor Brewery was owned by Henry Pointer. Rowe's *Illustrated Cheltenham Guide* described it thus: 'Those who have not yet followed the precepts of Father Matthew, and eschewed John Barleycorn and the other creature comforts, a moderate use of which "maketh glad the heart of man", an establishment like Mr Pointer's, noted for the purity of its "home-brewed" is one which ensures ready patronage'.

Right: An 1850 advert gave the price of Dowle's beers at the Carlton Brewery in Hewlett Street as 'X at 8d & 10d per gallon, XX at 1s, 1s 4d & 1s 6d per gallon and XXX at 1s 8d & 2s per Gallon'. Presumably their customers chose the cheapest option. The Carlton Brewery was acquired by Charles Garton & Co. of Easton Road, Lawrence Hill, Bristol.

Below: The Beehive in Montpellier Villas once brewed its own beer. An 1851 advert describes the proprietor J. Carter as a 'wine and spirit merchant and genuine ale brewer. Families supplied with genuine home-brewed ale and beer in large or small casks and sent to any part of the town. Dealer in malt and hops'.

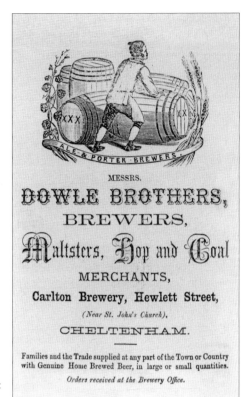

MESSRS.

DOWLE BROTHERS,
BREWERS,

Maltsters, Hop and Coal

MERCHANTS,

Carlton Brewery, Hewlett Street,

(Near St. John's Church),

CHELTENHAM.

Families and the Trade supplied at any part of the Town or Country with Genuine Home Brewed Beer, in large or small quantities.

Orders received at the Brewery Office.

THE STRAND   CHELTENHAM

Left: Whitbread took an interest in the real-ale revival of the early 1980s and established a small brew plant inside the Old Swan Hotel in Cheltenham in 1983. Unfortunately the Old Swan beers were made with malt extract instead of traditional pale malt. Beer drinkers were not impressed with the resultant syrupy flavour and the brewery had closed down by 1987.

Below: Regulars in the Apple Tree Inn, Woodmancote enjoying Cheltenham-brewed ale, *c.* 1958. Included here are: Reg Compton, Bill Jones, Ginger Scattergood, Frank Rowe, Johnny Lehane, Bill Jukes, Con Little, Peter Finch and Fred Larner. The gentleman on the right appears to have developed the knack of balancing a plate of sandwiches on his head!

three

Stroud Area
Breweries

GODSELL & SONS

TRADE MARK.

PALE ALE and STOUT BREWERS.

An excellent **LIGHT DINNER ALE (AK)**, at 1/- per gallon,
brewed specially for the private family trade.

NOURISHING STOUT, at 1/4 per gallon.

Salmon's Spring Brewery, STROUD.

Branches—CHELTENHAM: 4, Regent Street;
GLOUCESTER: The Cross, 47, Eastgate Street.

'Godsell & Sons Ale is brewed from the very purest spring water drawn from a spring within the sight of the brewery, and from the very finest malt and hops. Every process of the preparation and delivery is carefully watched and scientifically safe-guarded. This ale contains a great deal of nutriment, is an undoubted aid to digestion, and has an excellent aroma, in addition to being a brilliant, sparkling fluid, delicious in itself as well as a healthy beverage.' *New Stroud Directory* advertisement, 1909.

Above: This scene, from around 1900, is possibly on the 50th anniversary of the establishment of Godsell's Brewery. The horse-drawn transport was overseen by Mr Edward Godsell, who lived at Salmon Springs House (AD 1698) seen in the background to the right of the telegraph poles.

Right: Godsell & Sons were taken over by the Stroud Brewery Co. in March 1928 with 'keen buyers and sellers on both sides'. The closure of Godsell's Brewery enabled the transfer of the bottling and processing plant to the Salmon Springs site and relieved space for brewing at the crowded Stroud Brewery site.

Above: The old Godsell & Sons malthouse at Salmon Springs is now in use as a furniture store. The Royal Mail sorting office located to the rear of the malthouse was the site of the brewery buildings.

Left: The distinctive Godsell's trademark of a malt shovel clasped in a hand with the Latin motto *Labore et Honore* can still be seen on the stonework of the old brewery offices fronting Stratford Park (see previous page). The trademark can also be seen on a few pubs: Greyhound, Stroud; Golden Heart, Tredworth; Wellington Inn and New Pilot, Gloucester.

In June 1905 the Licensing Committee reported that in Albion Street there was 'the biggest cluster of licensed houses in Cheltenham with seven ale houses and five beer houses'. After frequenting some of these hostelries the 'hot dinners, daily chops and steaks' available at the Vine Tree 'at the shortest notice' must have been most welcome indeed.

The Royal William at Cranham had a dubious reputation several centuries ago when it was frequented by 'charcoal burners, gypsies, freebooters, smugglers and others of doubtful calling'. Things had improved by the 1920s when Godsell & Sons of Stroud owned the inn. Godsell's Brewery also supplied beer to the nearby Adam & Eve Inn at Paradise, a mile down the road. A sign outside said: 'Adam & Eve, Paradise – God Sells Beer!'

Left: Upon refurbishment by Godsell & Sons, in the early part of the last century, the Green Dragon in King Street, Stroud, boasted an ornate patterned façade with stained glass and etched brewery windows. The interior of the Green Dragon was probably just as stunning with ornate mahogany bar fittings, decorative tiling, and snob screens. The building is now occupied by Halfords.

Below: The Cross Hands in Brockworth was a home-brew pub in 1856. The pub was sold to William Sadler Hall of Cranham in 1875 who operated a small brewery at the Royal William Inn. Godsell & Sons of Salmon Springs bought the Cranham Brewery in 1914. Stroud Brewery acquired Godsell's and the Cross Hands Inn in 1928. A brand new pub was opened on 13 December 1937 and still trades today.

The Five Alls in Cheltenham's Upper Bath Road was another pub that once sold beer from the Cranham Brewery. The painted lettering on the pub's exterior is a credit to the Godsell's signwriters; Cranham Ales are still advertised in the pub window.

The Church Street Brewery bottling department, seen in a flurry of activity. At the time the photograph was taken, the building was used by Fawke's Stores. Previous, mid-century brewers were C. Jones and Charles James, but the most successful occupiers were Holmes, Harper and Neame, with twenty-one tied houses. The company also ran the Grey's Brewery in Henley, but by 1893 the brewery in Stroud was up for sale.

Above left: A recent photo of the ex-premises of the Uplands Brewery in Middle Street. The building was a shop for over 100 years and, along with some red-brick outbuildings to the rear, was used as a small brewery in the late nineteenth century. The delivery horses were stabled further up Middle Street to the rear of Lavender Cottage.

Above right: Mrs Caroline Guildford – her name was mis-spelt on the stone jar – was listed as being a shopkeeper and beer retailer at Uplands Brewery between 1889 and 1902. The Uplands Brewery was a very small concern, although Mrs Guildford did try to expand her business by bottling mineral water.

Opposite above: Alan Neame from the Church Street Brewery moved onto his own concern, the Eagle Brewery at Bowbridge in 1892. In this wonderful axonometric advertisement, the brewery is seen to dominate the locality. In reality, it occupied an old mill building (Eagle Mill) and a few sheds. The offices still survive, along from the British Oak pub.

Opposite below: Portly Alan Neame, the jovial brewer, was up against heavy competition from the outset. On the front of Stroud newspapers in the 1890s, there were often adverts from six local breweries – all trying to outdo each other. Insufficient outlets were found and, in 1897, the Eagle Brewery was acquired by the Nailsworth Brewery, of whom Alan Neame became a director.

An advertisement in the *Stroud Valley Illustrated* proclaimed that 'the name of the firm Carpenter & Co. is a synonym for the delicate high class Pale Ales, in the production of which purity and excellence are the chief watch words'. The Cainscross Brewery brewed almost entirely for the family trade. Its Family Pale Ales were said to be 'brilliant and sparkling, delicate in aroma, appetising to the palate, giving tone to the constitution'.

The brewing water at the Cainscross Brewery was obtained from a deep spring 'from a distant hillside which pours a continuous crystal stream into a tank at the top of the brewery'.

The Cainscross Brewery was put up for sale on 27 April 1926. The particulars of sale stated that the brewery had a fourteen-quarter mash tun and a forty-barrel copper. If Carpenter & Co. brewed just three times a week they would have had to sell over 4,000 gallon jars to their customers each week!

An advertisement for Carpenter & Co.'s Cainscross Brewery in the *Stroud and District Directory* of 1909 stressed that their beers were 'for the better classes'.

Left: Carpenter & Co.'s Cainscross Brewery Mild, Pale Bitter Ales and Stout could be 'obtained in casks of all sizes, screw-stopper bottles and jars conveniently fitted with stopper and tap'.

Below: Although the True Heart in Frampton on Severn was seven miles away from Cainscross it was the only tied house of Carpenter & Co. Thomas Hawker was the landlord of the pub in 1903.

In 1895 Cordwell & Bigg, the brewers at the Hamwell Leaze Brewery at Cainscross, could not sell beer to the public in quantities of less than four-and-a-half gallons (a pin). An application was put to the police to alter the licence so the brewery could sell smaller quantities of beer but it was refused on the grounds that there were other licensed premises nearby.

Tom Cordwell, brewery owner, is seated with his wife, Ann, in the centre of this family photograph, c. 1900. Their sons and daughters, from left to right: Lilian (seated), Harold, Millicent, Lionel, Ewert, Irene. Mr L.C. Cordwell was brewer at the Hamwell Leaze Brewery in 1914. Lionel was also the founder of the Cordwell's motor garage in Ebley, Stroud.

Cordwell & Sons went bankrupt in 1907 but a new company was formed which supplied the free trade from Tewkesbury to Bristol. Due to a shortage of staff brewing came to an end in around 1940 but Cordwell's continued to operate as beer bottlers until 1957, mainly for Watney's.

Brimscombe Brewery pubs were mostly concentrated within the Stroud Valleys. However, they supplied a few pubs in Gloucester (Dolphin, Northgate Street; Nelson Inn, Southgate Street; Welsh Harp, London Road), and had a few outlets in the Cirencester area (Three Horseshoes, Cricklade Street; Good Intent, Cerney Wick; Queens Head, Fairford, and Pig and Whistle, Quenington).

Staff outside the Brimscombe Brewery, c. 1913. Fourth from the left is Bill Fisher, who later became a drayman for Stroud Brewery Co. The First World War was soon to severely restrict the amount of hours pubs could open. The beer duty per standard barrel rose from 7s 9d to 23s, rising again to 50s in 1918. No wonder that so many breweries closed during this period.

The proprietor of the Victoria Hotel in 1906, Henry Eddels, ran a horse-drawn transport business. Every Thursday, during the summer months, he offered excursions to 'Framilode, Birdlip, Cirencester Park and other places of interest'. Henry could even supply a four-horse charabanc for ball or pleasure purposes.

William Lewis was the landlord of the Clothiers Arms in Chalford at the time of this photograph, *c.* 1903. The name changed to the Valley Inn on 11 February 1916. The Valley Inn finally closed in 1969. Smith & Sons' Brimscombe Brewery also owned the Fleece Inn on Chalford Hill.

Painswick.
Bell St. Gables &c.

Above: Although it was no longer a pub, the old Bell Inn met a spectacular fate on the night of the 14/15 June 1941 when a stray German bomb totally demolished the building. The Luftwaffe crew is thought to have mistaken Painswick for the Gloster Aircraft Co. at Brockworth. Ironically, two evacuees died in the air raid.

Right: When the Brimscombe Brewery was put up for sale in 1915 it was described as a modern brewery with an up-to-date brewing plant with twenty-two freehold hotels and two leasehold licensed premises. The twenty-two pubs raised £18,075 – a bargain at £821 each! The brewery was not sold until four years later when it was acquired by the Stroud Brewery Co.

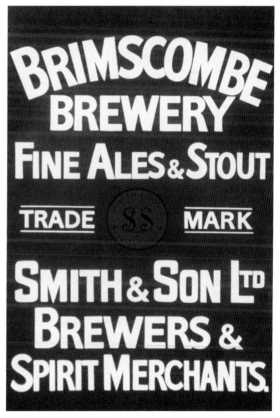

CHANCERY DIVISION

Mr. JUSTICE YOUNGER.

Re SMITH & SON, LIMITED.

SMITH v. SMITH & SON, LIMITED.

GLOUCESTERSHIRE and WILTSHIRE.

Particulars and Conditions of Sale

OF THE

BRIMSCOMBE BREWERY

NEAR STROUD, comprising

A MODERN BREWERY

(10 quarters), fitted with thoroughly up-to-date Brewing Plant,
15-quarter Malt House, Bottling Store, etc.,

22 FREEHOLD HOTELS AND LICENSED PREMISES

And Two Leasehold Licensed Premises

which

HENRY TEW BRUTON

Will, pursuant to an Order dated the 22nd July, 1915, SELL BY AUCTION

At the BELL HOTEL, GLOUCESTER,

ON WEDNESDAY, SEPTEMBER 22nd, 1915,

AT 3 O'CLOCK PUNCTUALLY, IN LOTS.

Particulars and Conditions of Sale may be had of Mr. R. E. STUART, Solicitor, Stroud, Glos.;
Mr. FRANK TREASURE, Solicitor, Gloucester; Messrs. PEACOCK & GODDARD, Solicitors,
3, South Square, Gray's Inn, W.C.; Messrs. WILLIS & WILLIS, Solicitors, 59, Chancery
Lane, W.C.; Messrs. SMITH, BAKER & PRICE, Accountants, Gloucester; or of the AUCTIONEER,
Albion Chambers, Gloucester (Telephone 967).

A bill of sale for Brimscombe Brewery, 1915. (Courtesy of Gloucestershire Record Office
D1405/4/357)

four

Southern Gloucestershire Breweries

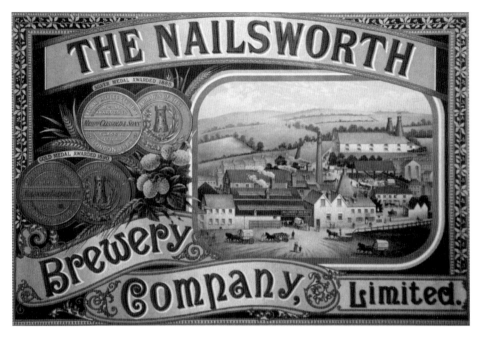

The fierce rivalry between the Stroud Brewery and the Cheltenham Brewery was evident in 1905 when the Nailsworth Brewery was being considered for possible takeover by the Stroud Brewery. The accountants had come to the conclusion that although the purchase of the Nailsworth Brewery was not necessarily a sound financial investment 'it may be politic to make some sacrifice to prevent the business from being acquired by a near neighbour'.

The Nailsworth Brewery was founded by Messrs Joseph and Samuel Clissold. Samuel died in 1842 and the brewery was carried on by Joseph Clissold. Mr W.G. Clissold, Joseph's son, then joined the business. Under the name of Clissold & Son the brewery became a successful concern and after further expansion a Limited Liability Company. Nailsworth Brewery was famous for its stout which could be supplied in 108-gallon casks!

In the year ending 31 March 1906 the Nailsworth Brewery spent £1,489 9s 4d on 'horse keep and travelling expenses'. The horse-drawn brewery dray is seen here at the King's Head in Upton St Leonards, 11 miles from the brewery. The brewery horses obviously worked very hard but who claimed the travelling expenses?

A Dursley 'pub crawl' in 1903 would almost certainly have included the King's Head and the Lamb Inn where Nailsworth Brewery ales and stouts could be sampled. The Nailsworth Brewery was amalgamated with the Cheltenham Original Brewery in 1908. Stroud Brewery had cause for concern as their main rival had secured a deal which brought Cheltenham Ales right into their own territory.

The profits of the Nailsworth Brewery decreased from £2,829 in 1906 to £1,978 8s 5d in 1907. In the year ending 31 March 1906 £1,283 13s 5d was spent on 'repairs to the brewery and public houses'. Charles Hurn, the landlord in 1906, had to pay £10 a year in rates at the Foston's Ash Inn near Birdlip. However, he had money left over for a new waistcoat and hat.

LOT 1.

THE VALUABLE AND EXTENSIVE PREMISES,

HITHERTO OCCUPIED AND KNOWN AS

THE FORWOOD BREWERY.

The main building of the Brewery comprises a Vat Cellar, 114ft. 6in. × 18ft. 6in., a Racking Cellar, 70ft. × 18ft. 6in., a smaller Racking Cellar, a second Vat Cellar, 30ft. 6in. × 19ft., and Fermenting Room ; on the first floor, a Hop Room, 52ft. 6in. × 18ft. 6in., Cooler and Hop Back Room, Engine Room and Boiler House, Wort Copper and Mash Tun Room, Tank and Feed Copper Room, Landing Stage, and Cask Washing Shed ; and also a Carpenter's Shop over Vat Cellar, 31ft. × 20ft. 6in.

THE BARLEY STORES

Comprise a Building of 3 floors, 37ft. 9in. × 18ft.

The main Building and the Barley Stores are connected by a Malt Grinding House and Chaff Cutting House and Stores.

Near to the Barley Stores is a Cow Shed for tying up 5 cattle, with Loft over.

THERE ARE FOUR MOST SUBSTANTIALLY BUILT MALTHOUSES.

No. 3—the one nearest the Brewery—has a cement ground floor, at one end of which is a stone wetting cistern with water supply, 87ft. × 18ft. ; a first floor, also cement and of similar dimensions, and above this a truck run. The Kiln has a tiled floor.

Each of the Malthouses, Nos. 1 and 2, contains two floors, with Malt Store and Kiln, with tiled floor.

The dimensions of the ground floor of No. 1 are 56ft. 9in. × 36ft. 9in., with stone wetting cistern and cement floor. The first floor is 56ft. 9in. × 17ft. 3in., with cement floor, and a Malt Store, 56ft. 9in. × 17ft. 8in. The third story is divided into bins.

Attached to No. 1 Malthouse is a Coopers' Shop.

No. 2 Malthouse contains two floors, each 80ft. 6in. × 17ft. 4in., the ground floor having a stone wetting cistern with water supply.

No. 4 Malthouse consists of three floors, the ground and first floors being 77ft. × 18ft. 5in., each having a concrete floor, and the ground floor having a stone wetting cistern. The top floor is divided into bins, a wire Kiln, and General Store Room.

The other Buildings comprise a double Coach-house, a Cart Shed, with Loft over, two-stall Stable, Stable for 7 horses, with Loose-box and Chaff-house attached thereto and a Loft over, a lean-to Shed for tying up 11 cattle, with a Storehouse adjoining.

The Buildings throughout are very substantially built of stone, most of the walls being 2 feet in thickness.

There is an abundant unfailing supply of excellent water.

The Property is about 2a. 1r. 0p. in extent, has important frontages of 330 feet and 370 feet respectively to the two main roads leading from Minchinhampton to Ball's Green, and offers exceptional advantages to a manufacturing firm or a public company.

The Property is sold subject to the condition that no brewing shall be carried on upon the premises, and also to the reservation of a portion of the practically inexhaustible water supply, but leaving ample supply for manufacturing or other purposes.

George Playne's Forwood Brewery in Minchinhampton was acquired by the Stroud Brewery in 1897 with thirty pubs, including the Black Horse at Amberley and the Crown Hotel in Minchinhampton. It is said that the Playne family once kept a pet monkey who caused havoc in the brewery when it was left unattended one day. Apparently the monkey turned the tap on a fermentation vessel and all the beer spilled out.

Opposite below: Joyce and Ernie Moss celebrate Pig Face Day at the Bell Inn, Avening, a Stroud Brewery pub, in 1950. This ancient celebration goes back to 1080 when Countess Matilda, wife of William the Conqueror, gave a feast of a boar's head. Nearly 900 years later, Joyce and Ernie gave away over 1,000 sandwiches cut from twelve pigs' heads. The feast drew hungry revellers from Bristol, Bath, Birmingham and London.

Cook's Tetbury Brewery was acquired by the Stroud Brewery Co. on 30 September 1913. Thirty-three public houses were included in the purchase including the King's Arms at Didmarton and the Red Lion at Ampney St Peter. The Tetbury Brewery continued brewing for a short time after the takeover while the capacity of the Stroud Brewery at Rowcroft was increased to meet the extra demand for beer.

Tetbury from Bath Road.

Robert Warn had established a brewery in Tetbury by 1776. In 1816 John Warn was brewing in Church Street. William Warn then took over the business. The brewery chimney had a brass steam whistle fitted to warn the residents of Tetbury of possible Zeppelin attacks in the First World War. Warn's Barton Steam Brewery went into liquidation in 1931 and was purchased by the Stroud Brewery.

Warn & Sons staff in April 1928. Charles Warn (seated front row centre) ran the brewery then and was also the fire brigade captain. An advertisement for Warn's Beer declared that it was 'arsenic free' which was a reference to an outbreak of poisoning in Salford in 1900 which killed 70 people and affected 6,000 others. The source was found to be from contaminated sulphuric acid used by some breweries.

The Trouble House Inn, two miles to the north-east of Tetbury, was once tied to Warn & Sons' Barton Brewery. In this postcard view the pub sign advertises 'Warn's Tetbury Ales.' The Trouble House Inn was purchased by Wadworth & Co. of Devizes, Wiltshire around 1937. The pub has a fascinating history: it was the scene of two suicides and has at least one resident ghost.

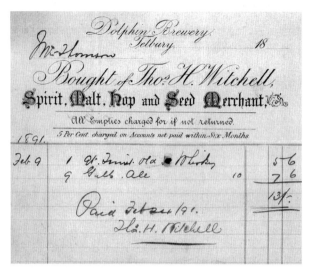

Left: Thomas Henry Witchell founded the Dolphin Brewery in Church Street, Tetbury, *c.* 1820. He was married to Mary, daughter of brewer John Warn. In 1903 the two neighbouring family breweries amalgamated. Witchell's brewed mainly for the family trade but they did have at least one tied house. The Fleece Inn at Hillersley was tied to Witchell's Dolphin Brewery in 1891 and 1903.

The Uley Brewery was established in 1833 by Samuel Price. At that time Uley was a thriving centre of the woollen industry and there were thirteen mills in the valley. Workmen at Uley were described as 'drunken and immoral – they never save one farthing'. The industry, however, was on the decline and within ten years the mills had closed. Samuel Price's son took over the ailing brewery.

Above: In 1984 the old brewery at Uley was put on the market and was purchased by Chas Wright. Within a year brewing had recommenced. The first beer was called UB 40 – Uley Bitter 4.0 per cent ABV. Chas is now brewing to capacity (fifty barrels a week) and brews Bitter, Old Spot, Pigs Ear, Laurie Lee's Bitter, and a new beer – Harping Hog.

Right: The Rt Revd Michael Perham, Bishop of Gloucester, made a brief visit to the Uley Brewery on 1 December 2004. The visit was part of the bishop's 'getting to know you' tour of Dursley. Hannah Curry, spokeswoman for the bishop, said the purpose of the visit was to give him a flavour of the area.

The Coombe Valley Brewery Co. near Wotton-under-Edge may have won a prize medal at the 1903 brewer's show but ran into financial difficulties soon afterwards. A receiver was appointed in 1908 and it seems that the brewery had closed by 1914, as the building was being used for mineral water manufacture. The licence to sell beer at the premises lapsed in 1918.

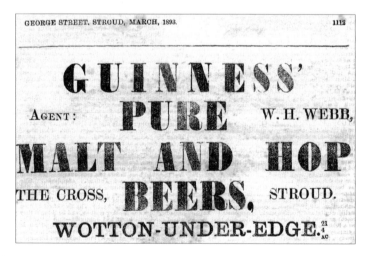

GEORGE STREET, STROUD, MARCH, 1893.   1113

GUINNESS'
AGENT: PURE   W. H. WEBB,
MALT AND HOP
THE CROSS, BEERS,   STROUD.
WOTTON-UNDER-EDGE.²¹⁄₄

By 1889, the Coombe Valley Brewery was established and managed by Arthur H. Guinness. Famed for its Double Stout, this brew, however, never challenged the national dominance of its namesake from Dublin. Deliveries were made to Frampton, Chalford and other free houses. Early in the twentieth century, the brewery was continued by Maj. Annersley and then by Sidney Underhill, who renamed it the Dawn of Day Brewery Co.

The buildings and chimney of the Bournstream Brewery are visible to the rear of the house. The right side of the house contained the Brewery Tap, a two-roomed ale house that opened straight onto the road. The premises were leased by the Perrett family from 1846, originally to David Perrett. Tied houses included the Anchor, Thornbury, and the Beaufort Arms, Hawkesbury Upton (CAMRA Gloucestershire Pub of the Year 2004).

When David Perrett died in 1869, his two sons Henry and Absolom continued the Bournstream Brewery. In 1887, Absolom sold his share to Henry who lived at the House. He is seen here with his family on the occasion of his fifty-second birthday, 26 July 1890. Just before this, the brewery was sold to Arnold & Co. of Wickwar and brewing was transferred there. The brewery was demolished in the late 1920s.

Left: In 1903 the New Inn at Waterley Bottom was tied to the Rock Brewery. Mary and Alf Moon kept the pub from February 1933 to September 1973. Earlier on there were spittoons under the benches and only one oil light on the wall. On horizontal bars by the fireplace, men would hang tankards of cider to warm it up. Every Saturday night, there was a sing-song, with each man singing the same song each week.

Below: By 1846 Mr Bloxome had set up a brewery in an old cloth mill near the Broadwell in Dursley. In 1867 the business was conducted by Bloxome & Cullen. In 1885 the brewery had closed. It was replaced by a row of terraced houses running up Bull Pitch from Water Street.

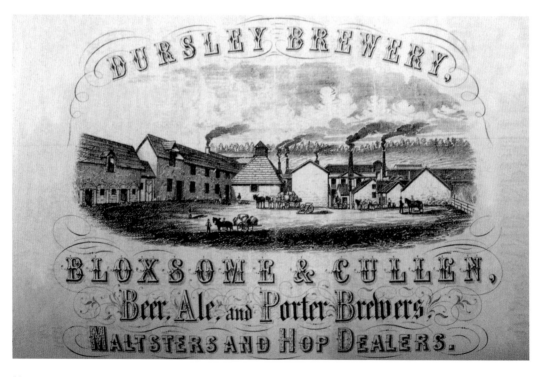

Union Street, Dursley

Thomas William Elvy's Brewery is visible at the bottom of Union Street and Boulton Lane in this postcard view of Dursley. After declaring bankruptcy in May 1906 the final brew at the Dursley Steam Brewery took place in April 1907. Perhaps Elvy's beers were not regarded in very high esteem by their customers. Poor quality malt and hops or a yeast infection could have easily ruined their reputation.

Right: The Dursley Steam Brewery was first established by a Mr C. Workman and then the business passed to Richard Chapman (1885), King & Worsley (1896) and latterly T.W. Elvy. Unfortunately contemporary photographs of the brewery have not been found for this book. The ginger beer stone jars represent the Dursley Steam Brewery under different periods of ownership. The larger Dursley Brewery Co. stone jar has no specified brewer.

The building to the left was the Cannonbury Brewery at Berkeley. In the nineteenth century, the Fear family carried on a cooperage business and a small brewery in outbuildings to the right. The door at street level led to the retail part of the brewery. Watering cans of beer were supposedly taken to the gardeners in the nearby Berkeley Castle. The Fear family made a sauce out of the waste brewing materials.

Dave McCredie started the Berkeley Brewery in 1994 in an eighteenth-century barn at Buckets Hill Farm. To begin with he brewed on a part-time basis but went full-time in 1997. On Thursday 3 August 2000 Dave was returning home from delivering beer in Wiltshire when he lost control of his van and hit a tree. Tragically, Dave died shortly afterwards at Princess Margaret Hospital, Swindon. (Courtesy of the *Gazette*)

BERKELEY BREWING CO.

The Legend of Dicky Pearce

It was the year 1728 and Dicky Pearce - England's last remaining Court Jester - was entertaining the Lords and Ladies at Berkeley Castle. Whether his performance that night wasn't up to scratch is not clear but tradition has it that Dicky was ejected over the balcony rail of the Great Hall by the fickle mob, plunging 20 feet to the floor below. As he lay battered and broken a callous attack by drunken revellers ensured his demise.

A Jesters tomb was erected in his memory and on the stroke of midnight on Halloween visitors to the edifice can place a penny piece on the tomb, run round it three times and hear the haunting laughter of Dicky Pearce as the penny disappears! So join us in a toast to Dicky - We're sure he would have loved to join you.

DICKY PEARCE

4.3% A HOPPY, FULL BODIED, BEST BITTER

THE BUCKETTS HILL BREWERY, BERKELEY, GLOUCESTERSHIRE
TEL: 01453 811895

Dave brewed two regular beers at the Berkeley Brewery: Old Friend, a 3.8 per cent golden beer and Dicky Pearce, a 4.3 per cent copper-coloured best bitter. Dave also brewed some occasional beers – Early Riser, Lord's Prayer, Late Starter, Severn Up, Bombers Moon and Jenners Cure. Dave McCredie was a cheerful and considerate man who is greatly missed.

Left: In 1891 the Arnold Perrett brewery was burnt to the ground. The fire broke out at midnight but the Chipping Sodbury brigade did not attend until 7 a.m. When the brewery was rebuilt after the fire it provided electricity for some street lighting in Wickwar. This was before the advent of mains electricity in the 1920s.

Below: Arnold Perrett & Co. were awarded two prize medals in 1885 for their beers. In 1895 they were brewing twelve different ales including milds, brown stouts, East India pale ale and strong ales. A kilderkin of their AKA bitter ale could be bought from the brewery for 21s.

Ray Penny and Brian Rides set up the Wickwar Brewing Co. in April 1990 in the old Arnold Perrett Cooperage. They had been tenants of Courage Brewery pubs and were disillusioned with only being able to stock certain beers. The new Wickwar beers were launched on the 'Glorious First of May 1990' (Guest Beer Order day).

The official opening of the new brewery at the old brewery in Wickwar took place on Friday 19 November 2004. Ray Penny and his brewing staff christened the new brewery by pouring bottles of their Cotswold Way over the mash tun. The new plant in the old Arnold Perrett & Co. brewery has a capacity of fifty barrels. The beers brewed using the new equipment have been absolutely superb.

Wickwar Gold Medal Ales are advertised on an enamel sign at the Plough Hotel in Bristol Road, Quedgeley, near Gloucester. In 1903 Arnold Perrett & Co. had at least 153 licensed premises in Gloucestershire.

The Original Gloucester Brewery was located in Westgate Street and extended into Quay Street. It was put up for auction on 7 October 1848. In 1889 Arnold Perrett & Co. acquired the wine and spirits business of James and Henry Hill who had bonded warehouses in Quay Street, possibly in the old brewery premises. Two Arnold Perrett lorries, Robin Hood and Friar Tuck, are seen outside the Gloucester depot.

Wickwar's other existing brewery, the Home County Brewery, was set up in 1997 by Steve Harker, in a renovated GWR parcel shed (built in around 1840). Brewing has been intermittent and was suspended after a flood several years ago. Possibly the smallest brewery in the area, it is hoped the brewery will expand in 2005. Beers such as Old Tradition and County Pride will be welcomed in more outlets.

GEORGE VIZARD & SON,

✦ STRONG BEER & ALE BREWERS, ✦
CHIPPING SODBURY.

LIST OF PRICES.
ALE, 6d. 8d. 9d. 10d. and 1/- per Gallon.
BEER, 1/2 1/3 1/4 and 1/6 " "

N.B. AGENTS FOR THE WEST OF ENGLAND FIRE AND LIFE INSURANCE OFFICES, ALSO THE RAILWAY PASSENGERS ACCIDENTAL ASSURANCE COMPANY.

Presented by _____

George Vizard & Son of Chipping Sodbury represent just one of the lesser-known common brewers. The High Street premises were later occupied by Hatherell Wines & Spirits.

This drawing depicts the Hill House Brewery at the top of Dog Hill, Old Sodbury. This once-distinctive landmark has been demolished but was sketched by Mr R.C. Pearce, a descendant of the Perrett brewing family. The brewery was operational by 1882, and had two tied houses – the Bell Hotel and Dog Inn, Old Sodbury and an off-licence in Chipping Sodbury. Brewing ceased in 1925.

Adam Bland, youngest son of cidermaker Vernon Bland, founded his brewery at a ramshackle cider mill at Oldbury-on-Severn in June 1980. He received great feedback from the Bristol Beer Festival and began to bottle his beers. Adam hoped to acquire a pub to sell draught beers but the dream was never realised. The brewing ceased later in 1980. Adam is now making traditional cider in France.

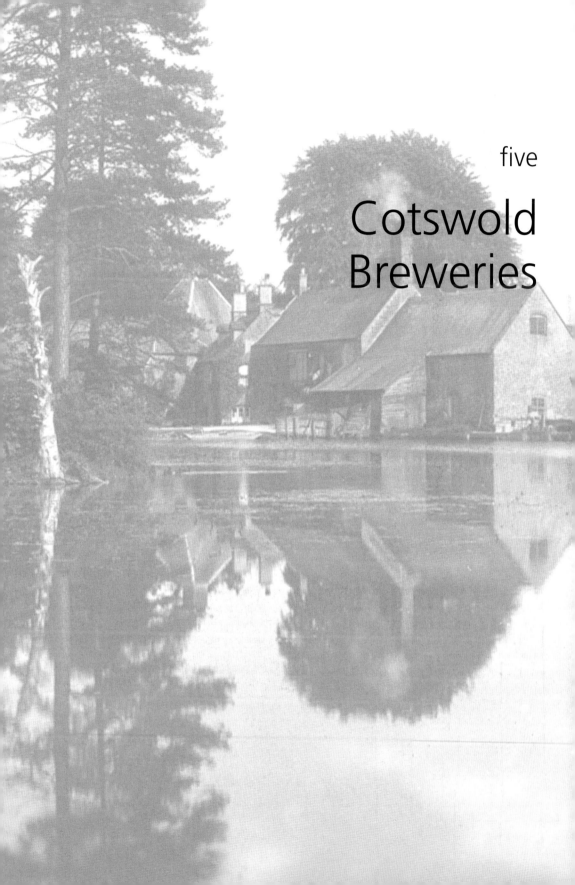

five

Cotswold Breweries

The Cirencester Brewery supplied beer to over sixty pubs in 1903. The majority of the tied houses were concentrated around the town of Cirencester and the surrounding villages but there were a few pubs in Cheltenham (Dukes Head, Duke Street; Royal Forester, Townsend Street and the White Swan, off Swindon Road).

Left: Cirencester Brewery workers were still happy in the 1930s, despite only having one bottle between them. From left to right, back row: Swan, Roseblade, Bushell, Drewett, Hitchings, –?–, Hewer, Rickards, Abbot. Front row: Griffiths, Plane, Stevens, Watts, Underwood, Weaving, Shayler.

Right: Cirencester beers and stout were available at the Black Horse until 1937 when the brewery was taken over by H & G Simonds of Reading. Miss Ruby Bower, the daughter of the landlord, reported seeing a ghost in her bedroom in 1933. Ruby woke up to see a woman in a long dress and apron, surrounded in a greenish light, approach her menacingly. The apparition then disappeared into a wall.

Below: The Bricklayer's Arms was built for the navvies working on the Thames and Severn canal. Mrs Annie Whiting was the landlady in 1906. The pub changed its name to the Daneway Inn and is still a popular pub today, although the canal has long since closed. An unusual pub game, Ring the Horn, is still played in the pub to this day.

THE BLACK HORSE
COMMERCIAL HOTEL, (opposite Post Office) CASTLE STREET,
CIRENCESTER.
PROPRIETOR, W. G. THORNTON.

CIRENCESTER BEER & STOUT.
BASS & Co's, BOTTLED ALE.   GUINNESS' STOUT.
GOOD ACCOMMODATION.

Henry Bliss was the landlord of the King's Head in Withington when this photograph was taken in 1900. He can be seen standing second from the right accompanied by his sons and daughters. The Cirencester Brewery supplied beers to the King's Head. The pub is still trading today, run by Mrs Coralie Taylor who was born in the building in 1929. Her parents had taken over the pub from Henry Bliss.

Brewing at the Cirencester Brewery came to an end in June 1937 when the business was acquired by H & G Simonds of Reading. Simonds Brewery was then taken over by Courage, Barclay & Co. in 1960. Most of the old Cirencester Brewery buildings in Cricklade Street were demolished. The words Cirencester Brewery Maltings can be seen on a building further down Cricklade Street which is now in residential use.

Edmund John Price was the landlord and brewer at the time of this 1909 advertisement: 'The Nelson Home Brewery (established over a century) is still brewing Pure Home Brewed Beer. These fine ales are used and recommended by the leading medical practitioners throughout the district as a pure and wholesome beverage.' The Nelson was probably the last home-brewed ales pub in Gloucestershire, and was still brewing in 1927.

Martin Bland and Shirley Harris set up the Cellar Brewery in the workshops at the Brewery Court, part of the Brewery Art Centre, and started trading in May 1983. The full-mashed beers were Cellar Bitter (1036 OG) and Cirencester Bitter (1040 OG). The name changed to the Cirencester Brewing Co. in 1986 and it closed in 1987. The Art Centre is the only surviving building of the Cirencester Brewery.

Built in 1847, the Butcher's Arms at Ampney Crucis once brewed its own beer. Mary Radway is recorded as a brewer there in 1891. The Stroud Brewery Co. purchased the pub and its brewery for £1,875 on 4 September 1899. The Butcher's Arms called last orders for the final time on 21 February 1997. It was a classic traditional pub with wood-block flooring and wooden seats.

At the turn of the twentieth century, Tayler & Co.'s Northleach Brewery supplied their Cotswold ales and stout to fifteen public houses. They had seven pubs in Northleach and Tayler & Co.'s beers could also be found in Aldsworth (Sherborne Arms), Moreton-in-Marsh (Swan Hotel), Fairford (White Hart), and one pub in Cheltenham (Dove and Rainbow, Burton Street).

After the Northleach Brewery had closed down the brewing copper was removed by winching it out of the building using a traction engine. Unfortunately the pipe work connecting the copper had not been properly removed. The traction engine toppled over under the strain but, luckily, the driver Hubert Blackwell escaped unscathed.

The valuation of the Northleach Brewery and its licensed houses was conducted in 1911. It concluded that the entire estate was worth a total of £18,145. The Compasses Inn in Withington was valued at £570 and was trading seventy-two barrels of beer a year. Tayler's Cotswold Brewery was acquired by the Cheltenham Original Brewery in 1919.

In the *Bennett's Business Directory* of 1908 Alfred Hadley & Sons are listed as brewers and maltsters in Sherborne Street, Bourton-on-the-Water. The malthouse with its distinctive pyramidal roof can be seen in this photograph. The brewery was located further down Sherborne Street in the grounds of Harrington House. Families were supplied with 4½-, 6-, 9-, 18- and 36-gallon casks.

The brewery at Harrington House was first established in around 1860 by a Mr Mills and Alfred Hadley bought it in around 1870. Harrington House itself was built in around 1740 and is one of the most imposing houses in the village being built on two storeys in a regional Palladian style. It seems that the brewery had closed by 1922 when the house was owned by J.A. Fort.

Right: The brewery office buildings, at the entrance to the Stow Brewery in Sheep Street, were built in 1869. On the upper floor was a Masonic Hall. The brewery was then owned by Richard and William Gillett. In 1885 the Stow Brewery had changed hands, and Greaves and Tusker are recorded as brewers. Edwin Augustus Green was the last owner of the Stow Brewery before it closed in 1914.

Below: In July 1898 a Mr W. Evans, an employee of Green's Stow Brewery, went to bed and in the middle of the night started sleepwalking. He walked straight through the bedroom window and fell onto the pavement below. He sustained cuts to his head and injured his foot. Apparently Green's Strong Bitter AK Ale was a particularly potent brew!

The Brewery Tap in Park Street was directly opposite the Stow Brewery and served as their tap house. Stow-on-the-Wold was a beer-drinker's paradise in Edwardian times. Donnington Beer was sold at the Queen's Head. Four Oxfordshire brewers supplied Stow pubs: Clinch's Eagle Brewery, Witney (Cross Keys); Hitchman & Co. of Chipping Norton (White Hart); Hunt Edmunds of Banbury (Kings Arms) and Hook Norton Ales (Wine Vaults).

The Sudeley Arms in Hailes Street was the only Stow Brewery pub in Winchcombe. Stow Brewery had sixteen tied houses in 1903 and the Sudeley Arms was the furthest from the brewery. The delivery of beer from the Stow Brewery to the Sudeley Arms by horse-drawn dray must have taken a whole day to accomplish. Not a job to be savoured in the cold, dark winter months.

Above: Once tied to Green's Stow Brewery, the Foxhill Inn (in an isolated position on the old Cheltenham to Stow road) closed in 1995. The old pub now offers bed and breakfast. On the outside wall is a Cheltenham & Hereford Ales ceramic plaque. Although similar in design to the West Country Ales plaques still seen on many Gloucestershire pubs this is the only known example of a Cheltenham & Hereford sign.

Right: In a quiet Cotswold valley, secluded and away from any village, the Donnington Brewery has often been described as the most beautiful brewery in Britain. The cluster of Cotswold-stone buildings stand next to an ornamental lake which is home to a variety of wildfowl and well stocked with rainbow trout. A water wheel provides power for the brewery.

Donnington was once a mill and was bought by Thomas Arkell in 1827. In 1865 Richard Iles Arkell started brewing there and was succeeded by his son Herbert. The present owner, Claude Arkell, took over from his father in 1952. Claude has no children to take over the business. When asked about the future he has said: 'It's in the hands of the Almighty. Nothing is certain except death and taxes'.

A brew run at the Donnington Brewery produces just eighteen barrels. The Flowers Brewery in Cheltenham could produce a staggering 2,000 barrels a day. The Donnington Brewery receive many requests for guided tours but this is not feasible because of the cramped conditions in the brew house and, perhaps more relevant, the brewery is located in private grounds.

The Donnington Brewery has fifteen tied pubs: Black Bear, Moreton-in-Marsh; Black Horse, Naunton; Coach & Horses, Ganborough; Coach & Horses, Longborough; Farmers Arms, Guiting Power; Fox Inn, Broadwell; Fox Inn, Great Barrington; Golden Ball, Lower Swell; Halfway House, Kineton; Mount Inn, Stanton; New Inn, Willersley; Plough Inn, Ford; Queens Head, Stow-on-the-Wold; Red Lion, Little Compton and the Snowshill Arms in Snowshill.

Donnington brew three traditional draught beers. Their popular BB is a pleasant amber bitter of 3.6 per cent ABV. SBA is a stronger, maltier, beer at 4.4 per cent ABV. They also brew a dark mild, XXX, which has an ABV of 3.6 per cent. This type of beer is not usually associated with Gloucestershire. Unfortunately XXX is brewed in very limited quantities. The Coach & Horses at Longborough usually stocks the excellent dark mild.

Above: When S. Knight was landlord, the
Golden Ball at Lower Swell was leased to
Richard Iles Arkell of the Donnington
Brewery. Amazingly, over 100 years later the
Golden Ball is still tied to the Donnington
Brewery.

Left: The Stanway Brewery was set up
in the Grounds of Stanway House near
Winchcombe in 1993 by Alexander
Pennycook. The brewery is housed in an
old brewhouse which was previously used
before the First World War to brew for the
house. The original large copper is still
used for the brewing of Stanney Bitter and,
uniquely, is fired by logs. (Courtesy of the
Gloucestershire Echo)

Opposite: Joseph Octavius Gillett is recorded
as a brewer at the Swan Hotel in Moreton-
in-Marsh in 1879. A gallon of XXXX
Strong Ale, 'guaranteed brewed from malt
and hops only', was available for 1s 6d.
Charles Gillett is listed as a brewer and
maltster in Moreton-in-Marsh in 1907 but
by this time the Swan Hotel was tied to
Tayler's Cotswold Brewery in Northleach.

CHAS. J. GILLETT

Awarded First-class Certificate and Bronze Medal by the
City and Guilds of London Institute, May, 1900.

(Late J. O. GILLETT.)

BREWER, ...

MALTSTER, ...

AND

SPIRIT MERCHANT,

MORETON-IN-MARSH

SPECIALITIES :

AK—Light Bitter Ale   ... **1 –** per gallon.

Ditto ... **2 6** per doz. Imperial pints.

Ditto ... **1 4**   ,,   ,, $\frac{1}{2}$ pints.

In screw stoppers or corks.

KX—Light Dinner Ale ... **10d.** per gallon.

Special Old Scotch Whisky, 42/= per doz.

Malt and Hops at Current Prices.

It is unclear when brewing took place at the North Street Brewery in Winchcombe. The existing corner buildings (now private houses) were built in around 1840. By 1896 the Nailsworth Brewery had a holding interest in the premises, which then passed to the Cheltenham Original Brewery in 1908. At the time, the North Street Brewery was used as a depot but carried on as an off-licence until the early 1950s.

There have been various attempts to scrub off the painted sign, but to no avail. The present inhabitants are happy to leave the sign even if it does attract the occasional thirsty tourist.

Right: Marcus and Alison Goff started brewing in Winchcombe in 1994. Regular beers include Tournament 1038 OG, Jouster 1040 OG, White Knight 1046 OG and Black Knight 1053 OG. The Goffs also brew seasonal ales under the title of Ales of the Round Table including Mordred, Launcelot, Guinevere, Galahad, Excalibur, Lamorak, Merlin and Camelot. Goffs Brewery supply bottled beer to the Gloucestershire Warwickshire Railway. (Courtesy of the *Gloucestershire Echo*)

Below: In the early 1900s the GWR were constructing the line from Cheltenham to Stratford-upon-Avon and the route passed through the village of Gretton. When the navvies were working on the nearby 693-yard-long Greet Tunnel they took liquid refreshment in the eighteenth-century Royal Oak. It was then free from brewery tie.

The Combe family acquired the Brockhampton Brewery near Andoversford in 1840 and it continued in family ownership until closure some eighty-seven years later. It is possible that the brewery was first established in 1769 as the date is inscribed into stone above a door opposite the brewery with the name I. Wood. In recent years the old tower brew house has been converted to residential use.

Left: When finding regular outlets for Brockhampton Brewery, draught beers proved to be difficult and the concept of packaging malt, hops and prepared yeast to sell as home-brew kits was developed by Reginald George Bradford Combe. These were available as early as the 1920s and were a forerunner to the familiar home-brew kits that are still popular today. Brewing ceased at Brockhampton in 1927 but the beer kits were made until 1939.

The kits contained 'Celebrated Cotswold Malt and Hops, with Yeast' and were sufficient to brew three gallons of beer for only 10½d. The wording on the packet read: 'If you possess a Brewer's Licence you may brew beer of any strength by reducing the quantity of water.'

Left: There is a brief reference to a W. Williams, brewer, in Fairview Street, Cheltenham, in 1856 and George Wheeler is recorded as a brewer at the Kemble Brewery Inn in 1883. By 1891 it was owned by Thomas Combe and beers were supplied from the Brockhampton Brewery. Combe's also supplied beer to the Plaisterer's Arms in Winchcombe. The Brockhampton Brewery was eventually sold to Ind Coope of Burton upon Trent.

Below: William Sadler Hall had established a small brewery at the Royal William Inn by 1891. He supplied seven other pubs with Cranham Ales: the Cross Hands in Brockworth and five Cheltenham pubs, Apple Tree, Russell Place; Crown and Cushion, Bath Road; Five Alls, Upper Bath Road; Gladstone Arms, Sherborne Street and the Sandford Inn, Sandford Street. The brewery was acquired by Godsell & Sons in August 1904 for £13,800

six

Gloucester, Tewkesbury and Forest Breweries

An advertisement in *Morris' Directory* of 1876 reads: 'Black Dog Inn. Agricultural and Commercial Inn & Brewery, Northgate Street, Gloucester. Centrally situated near the railway stations and the cattle market. Private sitting rooms. Agriculturalists, commercial gentlemen and visitors will find every convenience and attention.' In 1909 the pub and brewery was purchased for £4,800 by the Stroud Brewery Co. The Black Dog Inn was demolished in 1966. The black dog statue on top of the building has survived and is stored at the city Folk Museum.

Right: The Northgate Brewery (established in around 1857) stood 'partly in George Street and partly in the space near the Market Place at the junction of Northgate Street and Market Parade'. An early advertisement describes their Pale Bitter Ales as being 'in splendid condition, and of better quality than that of much of the so-called Burton at higher prices'. Ironically Hatton & Co. were acquired by Ind Coope of Burton upon Trent in 1896.

Below: When the Robin Hood Inn in Hopewell Street closed down in 1967 the Whitbread plyboard signs were removed to reveal the original raised lettering: Stroud Brewery Ales & Stout. The Robin Hood Inn was rebuilt by the Stroud Brewery in 1908 at considerable expense. Fortunately the wonderful green-tiled exterior can still be seen to this day.

NORTHGATE BREWERY,
GEORGE STREET,
GLOUCESTER.

----:❖:----

A. V. HATTON & CO.,

BREWERS OF

BITTER ALE,

MILD AND STRONG ALES,

Porter and Extra Stout,

Supplied in Casks, of 5, 9, 18, 36, and 54 galls. each.

These Ales are guaranteed Genuine, are unsurpassed in quality and defy competition.

----:❖:----

THE TRADE SUPPLIED

The Marquis of Granby,

BARTON STREET,

GLOUCESTER.

FREE HOUSE.

Proprietor: H. J. BICK.

ALTON COURT ALES.

MITCHELLS & BUTLER'S ALES.

DEWAR'S, WATSON'S, BUCHANAN'S, DUNVILLE'S
AND JOHNNIE WALKER'S WHISKIES.
"COURVOISIER" COGNAC the Brandy of Napoleon.

Above: The 1885 *Kelly's Directory* gives details of the Laburnham Brewery Inn and another reference in the 1906/07 *Matthew's Gloucester Directory* gives the address as No. 2 High Street, Tredworth. John Apperley is recorded as a brewer at the Laburnham Brewery. The beers were also available at the Beehive Inn, Millbrook Street. John Apperley is recorded as a brewer at the Laburnham Brewery in Ryecroft Street in 1895.

Left: Herbert Jonah Bick is recorded as the landlord of the Marquis of Granby between 1927 and 1939. Alton Court Ales were brewed in Ross-on-Wye and finally succumbed to the Stroud Brewery in 1956. Apparently Herbert's eight dogs had impeccable table manners!

The pub on the left-hand side of Eastgate Street is advertising 'Home Brewed Ales'. This is the Running Horse Inn which was run by Mrs L.A. Berry in 1906. It closed down a year later. In 1880 there were 12,417 pubs in England making their own beer but in 1914 there were just 1,447. The Bell Inn was tied to Godsell & Sons' Salmon Springs Brewery, Stroud.

On 3 May 1904 electric trams were introduced in Gloucester. In the first week of operation the trams carried 70,000 passengers and travelled 6,000 miles. No doubt some of the passengers had a crafty pint of Stroud Beer at the Admiral Benbow Inn. The pub was demolished some four years later, presumably because it was located right in the middle of Westgate Street!

Thornycroft Sturdy ZE/&RS Stroud Brewery dray No. 7 unloads bottles of beer and wooden casks of Cotswold Beers to the Olde Swan & Falcon in Longsmith Street, Gloucester. In May 1960 the pub's darts team set a new world record for scoring 1,000,001 which they achieved in seventeen hours and thirty-four minutes. The pub was demolished and the site is now occupied by a multi-storey car park.

One hundred years ago the Quay Street and Lower Westgate areas of Gloucester were a beer-drinker's paradise. The Globe in Quay Street was tied to Godsell & Sons but within a very short distance, beers could be drunk from the Nailsworth Brewery (Duke of Gloucester), Brimscombe Brewery (Elephant & Castle), Arnold Perrett & Co. (Ship, Old Dial), Cheltenham Brewery (Star), Wintle's Mitcheldean Brewery (Mermaid) and Stroud Brewery (Admiral Benbow).

In 1902 Godsell & Sons had thirty-nine public houses in Gloucester and Arnold Perrett & Co. had thirty-four. The Wickwar brewers thought it most unfair that sixteen of their city pubs had been referred to the Compensation Authority for closure, while their Stroud rivals had 'never had a single licence taken away'. The Kingsholm Inn continues to trade to this day.

Bob Readdie and Dennis Prenter started brewing in the Norfolk House Hotel in Bristol Road, Gloucester in October 1978. Four 60-gallon brews of Hawthorne Special Bitter (1042 OG) and Extra (1038 OG) were brewed a week, alternating between the two brews. It was hoped that the Hawthorne beers could be brewed in a Victorian grain store in Gloucester Docks but the plan never materialised. Hawthorne Brewery closed in 1983.

The Mayhem's brewery at the Farmer's Arms in Lower Apperley was established in August 1993 and brewed two beers, Oddas Light 3.8 per cent ABV and Mayhem's Sundowner 4.5 per cent ABV. In October 1997 the Farmer's Arms and its brewery was taken over by Wadworth of Devizes. The brewery closed in 2001.

Whittington's Brewery at the Three Choirs Vineyards in Newent was established in early 2003. The beers are Cats Whiskers (4.2 per cent ABV) and Nine Lives (3.6 per cent ABV). The beers are full-mashed and brewed by Kevin Shayle with the assistance of Ben Jennison.

Above: There were once two breweries in Tewkesbury located near the Borough Mills. Confusingly, they are both referred to at different times as the Tewkesbury Brewery. The Abbey Brewery was located along Smiths Lane and fronted the High Street. The brewery was owned by Joseph Jupp in 1890. When it closed the premises were used as a garage.

Right: The other Tewkesbury Brewery was once known as the Original Brewery and still exists in Quay Street, near Healings Mill. The words Tewkesbury Brewery and Blizard & Colman are still clearly visible. There is also a fine piece of ornamental plasterwork of a hand holding a sheaf of barley. In 1890 the Abbey Brewery merged with the Quay Street Brewery and was registered as the Tewkesbury Brewery Co. Ltd.

Above: This splendid photograph of the Black Bear in Tewkesbury's High Street was taken 130 years ago in 1875. The pub was tied to Blizard & Colman's Original Brewery in Quay Street. The Tewkesbury Brewery Co. was acquired by Arnold Perrett & Co. of Wickwar in May 1893. James Wilkes Wilson had taken over the business from Blizard & Colman at the time of purchase.

Left: Immediately to the rear of the Wheatsheaf Inn in Tewkesbury High Street stood Thomas Walker & Sons. This was a factory established in 1871 that specialised in building fairground equipment. No doubt some of the employees enjoyed a pint or two of Tewkesbury Brewery Ales at the Wheatsheaf after work. The classic black and white timber-framed building dating from the early sixteenth century ceased to be a pub in around 1939.

Immediately behind the Old Black Bear Inn, in what is now the riverside garden, once stood another brewery. Bayliss & Merrell, established 1750, were located near St John's Bridge. The business was mainly based on importing foreign wines and spirits but there was also a distillery and brewery on the premises. Bayliss & Merell were put up for auction in April 1921 and had closed by around 1924.

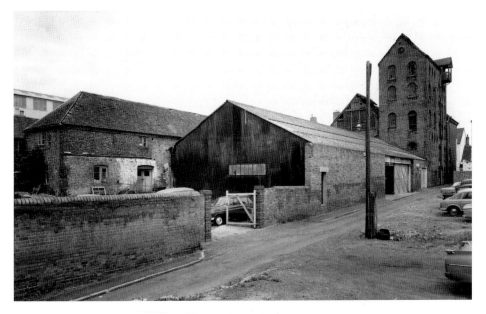

Bayliss & Merrell had only three tied houses: the Nottingham Arms, High Street, Tewkesbury; the Seven Stars, Upton-on-Severn and the New Inn (now the Village Inn), Twyning. After the bonded warehouse, brewery and distillery closed in around 1924 the buildings were converted to a dairy. This photograph shows the rear of the old Bayliss & Merrell brewery nearly forty years after closure.

The Stockwell Inn in Cinderford was a one-roomed beer house located down a 'bad road' opposite the cricket ground. It was tied to Francis Wintle's Forest Brewery in Mitcheldean. The landlord in 1903, Christopher Banks, apparently kept sheep and turkeys in the pub garden – perhaps he was partial to Sunday roasts! The Stockwell Inn was referred to the Compensation Authority in 1911.

The Hawthorn Brewing Co. in Steam Mills Road Cinderford was founded in October 1985 by Andrew Baber. It had closed by 1987. The Freeminer Brewery is now located within a stone's throw of the old Hawthorn Brewery.

In October 1992 Don Burgess established the Freeminer Brewery. It takes its name from the people who are born within the Hundred of St Briavels who have the right to freely mine minerals from the Royal Forest of Dean. Don takes a great deal of pride in Forest history and his beers are named after former mines in the area such as Deep Shaft and Shakemantle.

The Freeminer Brewery was originally located at the Laurels Industrial Park at Sling, near Coleford. In 2001 Don moved to the Whimsey Brewery in Steam Mills Road, Cinderford – a much larger brewery able to cope with the ever-increasing demand for his real ales in both cask and bottle. Freeminer Brewery has a contract with the Co-op to supply the excellent bottled conditioned beer, Gold Miner.

The Tump House Inn, just outside Blakeney, was a free house in 1891 but was likely to have sold beers from the local Blakeney Brewery. The inn was later acquired by the Stroud Brewery Co. The landlady in 1960, Mrs Francis Biddington, had been resident at the Tump House since 1904. Her father was James Reeves. The inn closed in the early 1970s.

The opening of the Severn Railway Bridge on 17 October 1879 enabled breweries on the other side of the River Severn easy access into the Forest of Dean. Arnold Perrett, Godsell, Nailsworth and Stroud Breweries all began to purchase pubs on the other side of the river. The Cross Inn in Aylburton was purchased by Godsell & Sons in around 1900 and became part of the Stroud Brewery tied estate in 1928.

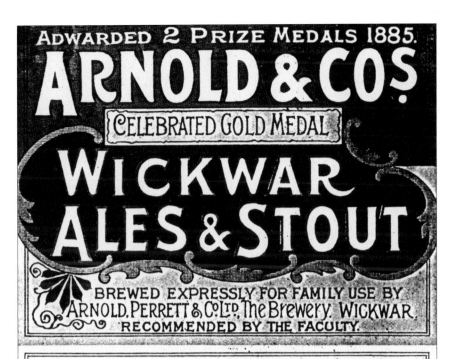

ADWARDED 2 PRIZE MEDALS 1885.

ARNOLD & CO'S

CELEBRATED GOLD MEDAL

WICKWAR ALES & STOUT

BREWED EXPRESSLY FOR FAMILY USE BY ARNOLD, PERRETT & CO LTD. The Brewery. WICKWAR. RECOMMENDED BY THE FACULTY.

Price List.

INDIA PALE AND BITTER ALES.

Brand on Cask.		Per Kilderkin.	Per Firkin.	Per Pin.
1	East India Pale Ale	27 –	13/6	6/9
2	Pale Ale	24/–	12/–	6/–
AKA	Bitter Ale	21/–	10/6	5/3
AK	,,	18/–	9 –	4/6

MILD ALES.

		Per Kilderkin.	Per Firkin.	Per Pin.
3	Mild Ale	15/–	7/6	3/9
4	,,	18/–	9 –	4/6
5	Burton Ale	21/–	10/6	5/3
6	Rich Mild Ale	24/–	12/–	6/–
7	Strong Ale	27/–	13/6	6/9
8	,,	30 –	15/–	7/6

STOUT.

		Per Kilderkin.	Per Firkin.	Per Pin.
BS	Brown Stout	21 –	10/6	5/3
DBS	Double Brown Stout	24 –	12 –	6 –

LOCAL OFFICES & STORES

HILL STREET, LYDNEY,

ALBION SQUARE, CHEPSTOW,

AND OLD BREWERY, BLAKENEY.

The Blakeney Brewery was also known as the Dean Forest Steam Brewery. In 1895 the brewery was operated by Samuel P. Evans & Co. and there were tied houses in Blakeney (Bird in Hand Inn), Coleford (Lamb Inn), Parkend (Railway Inn) and Viney Hill (Albion Inn). Arnold Perrett & Co. acquired the brewery and used the premises as their Forest of Dean depot.

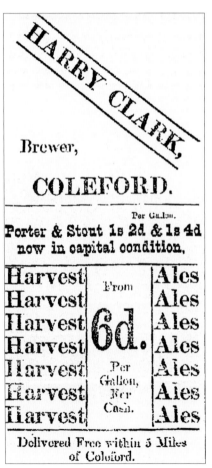

HARRY CLARK,

Brewer,

COLEFORD.

Per Gallon.

Porter & Stout 1s 2d & 1s 4d now in capital condition,

Harvest	From	Ales
Harvest		Ales
Harvest	**6d.**	Ales
Harvest		Ales
Harvest	Per Gallon,	Ales
Harvest	For Cash.	Ales
Harvest		Ales

Delivered Free within 5 Miles of Coleford.

Above: The Redbrook Brewery was founded in 1825. Oliver Arthur Burgham's Redbrook Brewery was acquired by Ind Coope of Burton upon Trent in 1923. Twenty-two public houses were included in the sale, including the Fountain Inn, Parkend; Lamb Inn, Clearwell; Ostrich Inn, Newland and the Prince of Wales, Sparrow Hill, Coleford.

Left: Brewers at The Spout, Coleford had come and gone in the early nineteenth century, but during the 1860s and '70s, this small brewery was run by Henry Salmon. By the time of this advert in 1885, Henry Clark was offering Harvest Ales from 6d a gallon (for cash!). The range of beers offered by the smaller county brewers depended on the passing of the seasons and is still mirrored today.

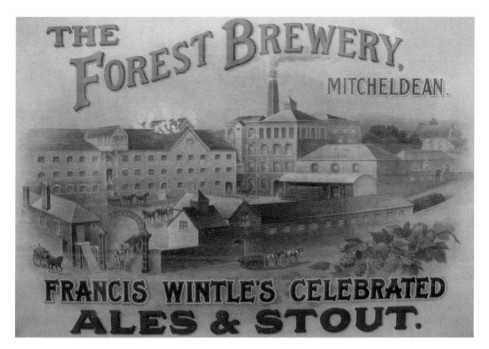

Thomas Wintle established a brewery at Mitcheldean in 1868. The supply of excellent brewing water from springs on the nearby sandstone hills was an important factor. The Forest Brewery used the finest Herefordshire barley and Worcestershire hops to make mild, bitter ales and stouts. The brewery was constructed of sandstone blocks from the local Wilderness Quarry and the premises eventually covered two acres of land.

When Thomas Wintle died in 1888 his son, Francis, took over the business. The Forest Brewery was one of the most modern breweries in the entire country. Interior walls were lined with white glazed brick to ensure absolute cleanliness, woodwork was painted to prevent the build-up of germs and hygiene was paramount. It is ironic that Francis Wintle had to retire due to ill health.

Wintle's Brewery suffered a devastating fire in 1926 when the roof of the malthouse was totally destroyed. The building was renovated after the fire but just four years later the Mitcheldean brewery was sold to the Cheltenham Original Brewery. In 1940 British Acoustic Films moved to the former Wintle's Brewery from London. In 1948 BAF was acquired by Rank Xerox who remained at Mitcheldean until the late 1990s.

The opening of the Severn Railway Bridge in 1879 and the Severn Railway Tunnel in 1886 enabled brewers from the Stroud Valleys and the Bristol areas easy access to the industrial Forest of Dean. The Forest Brewery in Mitcheldean did not purchase pubs in the agricultural Vale of Berkeley but the Wintle's Sentinel steam dray, pictured here at Cinderford station in 1900, proved that they did use the Forest railways.

Francis Wintle,

— THE BREWERY, —

MITCHELDEAN, GLOS.

Brewer, Maltster and Miller.

NOTED PALE ALE AND STOUT
supplied in casks of any size.

Flour Mills, Cinderford.

All communications should be addressed to

FRANCIS WINTLE,
The Brewery :: Mitcheldean.

When the Cheltenham Original Brewery acquired the Mitchledean Forest Brewery, and about eighty licensed houses for £250,000 in 1930, Mr K.O. Homfray, managing director of Wintle's Brewery Co. Ltd. 'exerted all his influence to persuade the new owners to continue brewing at Mitcheldean which employs about fifty hands.' Cheltenham Original Brewery closed the Mitcheldean brewery down exactly seven years later.

Other local titles published by Tempus

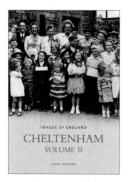

Cheltenham Volume II

ELAINE HEASMAN

Comprising over 230 rare postcards and photographs, this book provides a glimpse into the history of Cheltenham during the last 150 years. There are images of many of the town's well-known landmarks, including the Promenade, the Ladies' College and the Queen's Hotel, as well as surrounding areas such as Charlton Kings, Prestbury and Leckhampton.

0 7524 3085 8

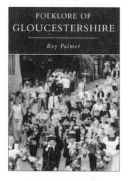

Folklore of Gloucestershire

ROY PALMER

Here are recounted tales inspired by landscape, village lore, legends, superstitions, stories of devils, fairies, witches and ghosts, sports and fairs, song and dance, revels and rituals. Roy Palmer is an acknowledged authority on the subject of folklore, and his work in collecting material from within the traditional boundaries of Gloucestershire is a major contribution to the historic records of the county.

0 7524 2246 4

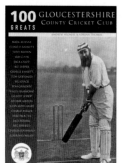

Gloucestershire CCC 100 Greats

ANDREW HIGNELL AND ADRIAN THOMAS

Gloucestershire CCC is steeped in tradition, with the history of the West Country club being richly decorated with some of English cricket's most famous names. Indeed, none could be larger than Dr W.G. Grace. This book proudly recalls the generations of illustrious players who have represented Gloucestershire and built on the record-breaking achievements of the immortal Doctor.

0 7524 2416 5

Haunted Gloucester

EILEEN FRY AND ROSEMARY HARVEY

Gloucester's historic docks have some strange stories to tell and the city's twelfth-century cathedral also has its secrets. From a ghostly procession at Berkeley Castle to the Grey Lady at the old Theatre Royal, this new and fascinating collection of strange sightings and happenings in the city's streets, churches and public houses is sure to appeal to anyone intrigued by Gloucester's haunted heritage.

0 7524 3312 1

If you are interested in purchasing other books published by Tempus, or in case you have difficulty finding any Tempus books in your local bookshop, you can also place orders directly through our website

www.tempus-publishing.com